1959 U.K.

YEARBOOK

ISBN: 9781792917592

This book gives a fascinating and informative insight into life in the United Kingdom in 1959. It includes everything from the most popular music of the year to the cost of a buying a new house. Additionally there are chapters covering people in high office, the best-selling films of the year and all the main news and events. Want to know which team won the FA Cup or which British personalities were born in 1959? All this and much more awaits you within.

INDEX

FIRST EDITION

1959

January

M	T	W	T	F	S	S
			1	2	3	4
5	6	7	8	9	10	11
12	13	14	15	16	17	18
19	20	21	22	23	24	25
26	27	28	29	30	31	

◗:2 ●:9 ◐:16 ○:24 ◑:31

February

M	T	W	T	F	S	S
						1
2	3	4	5	6	7	8
9	10	11	12	13	14	15
16	17	18	19	20	21	22
23	24	25	26	27	28	

●:7 ◐:15 ○:23

March

M	T	W	T	F	S	S
						1
2	3	4	5	6	7	8
9	10	11	12	13	14	15
16	17	18	19	20	21	22
23	24	25	26	27	28	29
30	31					

◗:2 ●:9 ◐:17 ○:24 ◑:31

April

M	T	W	T	F	S	S
		1	2	3	4	5
6	7	8	9	10	11	12
13	14	15	16	17	18	19
20	21	22	23	24	25	26
27	28	29	30			

●:8 ◐:16 ○:23 ◑:29

May

M	T	W	T	F	S	S
				1	2	3
4	5	6	7	8	9	10
11	12	13	14	15	16	17
18	19	20	21	22	23	24
25	26	27	28	29	30	31

●:7 ◐:15 ○:22 ◑:29

June

M	T	W	T	F	S	S
1	2	3	4	5	6	7
8	9	10	11	12	13	14
15	16	17	18	19	20	21
22	23	24	25	26	27	28
29	30					

●:6 ◐:14 ○:20 ◑:27

July

M	T	W	T	F	S	S
		1	2	3	4	5
6	7	8	9	10	11	12
13	14	15	16	17	18	19
20	21	22	23	24	25	26
27	28	29	30	31		

●:6 ◐:13 ○:20 ◑:27

August

M	T	W	T	F	S	S
					1	2
3	4	5	6	7	8	9
10	11	12	13	14	15	16
17	18	19	20	21	22	23
24	25	26	27	28	29	30
31						

●:4 ◐:11 ○:18 ◑:26

September

M	T	W	T	F	S	S
	1	2	3	4	5	6
7	8	9	10	11	12	13
14	15	16	17	18	19	20
21	22	23	24	25	26	27
28	29	30				

●:3 ◐:9 ○:17 ◑:25

October

M	T	W	T	F	S	S
			1	2	3	4
5	6	7	8	9	10	11
12	13	14	15	16	17	18
19	20	21	22	23	24	25
26	27	28	29	30	31	

●:2 ◐:9 ○:16 ◑:24 ●:31

November

M	T	W	T	F	S	S
						1
2	3	4	5	6	7	8
9	10	11	12	13	14	15
16	17	18	19	20	21	22
23	24	25	26	27	28	29
30						

◐:7 ○:15 ◑:23 ●:30

December

M	T	W	T	F	S	S
	1	2	3	4	5	6
7	8	9	10	11	12	13
14	15	16	17	18	19	20
21	22	23	24	25	26	27
28	29	30	31			

◐:7 ○:15 ◑:23 ●:29

PEOPLE IN HIGH OFFICE

Monarch - Queen Elizabeth II
Reign: 6th February 1952 - Present
Predecessor: King George VI
Heir Apparent: Charles, Prince Of Wales

United Kingdom

Prime Minister - Harold Macmillan
Conservative Party
10th January 1957 - 19th October 1963

Australia

Canada

United States

Prime Minister
Sir Robert Menzies
19th December 1949 -
26th January 1966

Prime Minister
John Diefenbaker
21st June 1957 -
22nd April 1963

President
Dwight D. Eisenhower
20th January 1953 -
20th January 1961

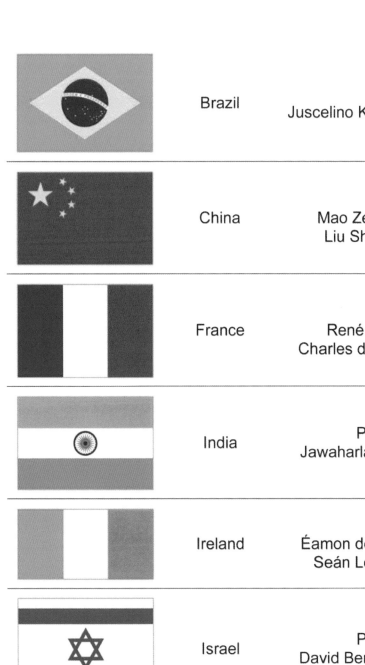

	Brazil	President Juscelino Kubitschek (1956-1961)
	China	Chairman Mao Zedong (1949-1959) Liu Shaoqi (1959-1968)
	France	President René Coty (1954-1959) Charles de Gaulle (1959-1969)
	India	Prime Minister Jawaharlal Nehru (1947-1964)
	Ireland	Taoiseach Éamon de Valera (1957-1959) Seán Lemass (1959-1966)
	Israel	Prime Minister David Ben-Gurion (1955-1963)

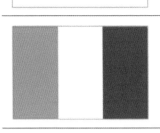

	Italy	Prime Minister Amintore Fanfani (1958-1959) Antonio Segni (1959-1960)

	Japan	Prime Minister Nobusuke Kishi (1957-1960)

Mexico

President
Adolfo López Mateos (1958-1964)

New Zealand

Prime Minister
Walter Nash (1957-1960)

Pakistan

President
Ayub Khan (1958-1969)

South Africa

Prime Minister
Hendrik Verwoerd (1958-1966)

Soviet Union

Communist Party Leader
Nikita Khrushchev (1953-1964)

Spain

President
Francisco Franco (1938-1973)

Turkey

Prime Minister
Adnan Menderes (1950-1960)

West Germany

Chancellor
Konrad Adenauer (1949-1963)

BRITISH NEWS & EVENTS

JAN

15th | The ITV franchise Tyne Tees is launched from studios at a converted warehouse in City Road, Newcastle upon Tyne.

1958 Formula One World Champion John Michael Hawthorn.

22nd January - Racing driver Mike Hawthorn is killed after his 3.4-litre Jaguar collides with a tree on the A3 near Guildford. Hawthorn had become the United Kingdom's first Formula One World Champion driver in 1958, whereupon he had announced his retirement after being profoundly affected by the death of his teammate and friend Peter Collins two months earlier in the 1958 German Grand Prix.

29th | Dense fog, the worst for seven years, brings road, rail and air transport in many parts of England and Wales to a virtual standstill. Although London is the worst affected many areas of the Midlands, East Anglia, southern England and east and south Wales are also shrouded in fog and frost for most of the day.

FEB

19th | The London and Zürich Agreements (for the constitution of Cyprus) are drafted and agreed, granting Cyprus independence from Britain. Cyprus was accordingly proclaimed an independent state on the 16th August 1960.

23rd | On the second day of his ten-day visit to the USSR, Prime Minister Harold Macmillan holds talks with the Soviet leader Nikita Khrushchev to expand Anglo-Soviet trade and cultural ties.

MAR

7th | Independence movement leader Kanyama Chiume, wanted in the British territory of Nyasaland (modern day Malawi), flees to London and goes into hiding.

10th | The comedy film 'Carlton-Browne Of The F.O.' starring Terry-Thomas, Peter Sellers and Luciana Paluzzi is released.

| 11th | The song 'Sing, Little Birdie', performed by husband-and-wife duo Pearl Carr and Teddy Johnson, comes second for the UK in the fourth ever Eurovision Song Contest. There would be four more second places for the UK at the contest finals before scoring its first Eurovision victory in 1967 with 'Puppet On A String' by Sandie Shaw. |
| 26th | Durrell Wildlife Park (now Jersey Zoo) is established by naturalist and author Gerald Durrell on the island of Jersey. |

Protestors march to London from Aldermaston to demonstrate their opposition to nuclear weapons.

30th March - The 1959 Aldermaston to London march, organised by Campaign for Nuclear Disarmament (CND), sees 20,000 demonstrators attend a rally in Trafalgar Square. This march followed the first major Aldermaston march at Easter 1958, which had been organised by the Direct Action Committee Against Nuclear War (DAC). The march became an annual event and at its height in the early 1960s attracted more than 100,000 thousand CND supporters.

APR

1st	The 'County Of Southampton' officially changes its name to the 'County Of Hampshire'.
2nd	United Dairies merges with Cow & Gate Ltd (of Guildford) to form Unigate Dairies.
22nd	The world famous British ballerina Dame Margot Fonteyn is released from prison after spending 24 hours in a Panama City jail. She had been suspected of involvement in a planned coup against the Panamanian government of President Ernesto de la Guardia.
23rd	London's first heliport, currently known officially as the NetJets London Heliport (previously called Battersea Heliport), opens for business. The facility, which was built by W. & C. French and located in Battersea on the south bank of the River Thames, is today London's only licensed heliport.
30th	Icelandic gunboats fire live ammunition at British trawlers over fishing rights during the first of the 'Cod Wars'.

MAY

Chapelcross nuclear power station on the day of its demolition - 20th May 2007.

2nd May - The Chapelcross nuclear power station in Dumfries and Galloway, Scotland, opens. It was the sister plant to the Calder Hall plant in Cumbria, England, and the primary purpose of its Magnox reactors was not only to generate electrical power for the National Grid but to produce weapons-grade plutonium for the UK's nuclear weapons programme. The plant was decommissioned in June 2004.

2nd	Nottingham Forest beats Luton Town 2-1 in the FA Cup final at Wembley Stadium.
7th	Scientist and novelist C. P. Snow delivers an influential Rede Lecture at the University of Cambridge on The Two Cultures, in which he laments the gulf between scientists and literary intellectuals. It provokes widespread and heated debate, and is subsequently published as 'The Two Cultures And The Scientific Revolution'.
24th	British Empire Day (the annual celebration of the Commonwealth of Nations held on the second Monday in March) is renamed Commonwealth Day.
28th	The Mermaid Theatre opens at Blackfriars in the City of London. It is the first to be built in the City since the time of Shakespeare and is also one of the first new theatres to abandon the traditional stage layout; instead a single tier of seats surrounds the stage on three sides.

1st | The BBC airs the music panel show Juke Box Jury, chaired by David Jacobs, for the first time. By 1962 the programme was attracting 12 million viewers weekly on Saturday nights, and an appearance on the 7th December 1963 by the Beatles garnered an audience of 23 million. It would run until the 27th December 1967, although the concept was later revived by the BBC for one series in 1979 and a further two series in 1989/1990.

3rd | Thirty-five year old Lee Kuan Yew is sworn in as the first Prime Minister of a self-governing Singapore. He remains as Prime Minister for over 31 years and his tenure leads to the expansion of Singapore's economy from a British Crown Colony into a first world country.

The SR-N1 hovercraft makes its first flight on the Isle of Wight in front of members of the press.

11th June - Christopher Cockerell's invention, the Saunders-Roe SR.N1 hovercraft, is officially launched and makes its maiden flight in front of various assembled members of the press. The demonstration received considerable press coverage, the majority of which being largely positive.

On the 25th July 1959, the 50th anniversary of Louis Blériot's cross-channel flight, the SR.N1 crossed the English Channel from Calais to Dover in just over two hours; the crew during this crossing consisted of Captain Peter Lamb (pilot), John Chaplin (navigator) and Cockerell himself.

In December 1959, the Duke of Edinburgh visited Saunders-Roe at East Cowes and persuaded the chief test-pilot, Commander Peter Lamb, to allow him to take over the SR.N1's controls. He flew the SR.N1 so fast that he was asked to slow down a little. On examination of the craft afterwards it was found that she had been dished in the bow due to excessive speed, damage that was never allowed to be repaired and was from then on affectionately referred to as the 'Royal Dent'.

JUN

22nd	Harrods enters talks with Debenhams over a possible £34m merger but The House of Fraser eventually went on to beat off the competition from Debenhams after raising its final price to acquire Harrods to £37m. The store returned to private ownership in 1985 when Mohammed al Fayed and his brother bought the House of Fraser for £615m - it is now owned by the state of Qatar.
23rd	Klaus Fuchs is released from Wakefield prison having served nine years and four months of a fourteen year sentence for giving British nuclear secrets to the Soviet Union. Having been stripped of his British citizenship he promptly emigrated to the German Democratic Republic and continued his scientific career. Fuchs went on to achieve considerable prominence as a leader of research in physics, nuclear and materials science.

JUL

	Cliff Richard and The Drifters earn their first No.1 record with the single 'Living Doll'. Written by Lionel Bart, the song became the top selling single in the UK in 1959. In aid of Comic Relief in 1986, Cliff, along with Hank Marvin and the Young Ones, re-recorded the single and it again reached the No.1 spot.
17	British paleoanthropologist Mary Leakey discovers the partial skull of a new species of early human ancestor, Zinjanthropus boisei or Zinj (now called Paranthropus boisei), that had lived in Africa some 1.75 million years ago.
28th	Postmaster General Ernest Marples announces that UK postcodes are to be introduced for the first time, as an experiment, in the city of Norwich.
29th	The Mental Health Act becomes law modernising the care of patients with mental disorders. The Act's main objectives are to abolish the distinction between psychiatric hospitals and other types of hospitals, and to deinstitutionalise mental health patients and see them treated more by community care. The Act repealed the Lunacy and Mental Treatment Acts 1890 to 1930 and the Mental Deficiency Acts 1913 to 1938.
29th	The Obscene Publications Act is given Royal assent, significantly reforming the law relating to obscenity in England and Wales. The Act created a new offence for publishing obscene material and allowed Justices of the Peace to issue warrants permitting the police to seize such materials.

AUG

26th August - The British Motor Corporation introduce the first Morris Mini-Minor, registration number 621 AOK. Designed by Alec Issigonis (pictured) the Mini was produced from 1959 until October 2000 (although BMW, after acquiring the Rover Group in 1994, have retained the rights to continue to build cars using the Mini name). The Mini is considered an icon of 1960s British popular culture and was voted the second most influential car of the 20th century behind the Model T Ford. In total 5.3 million Minis have been sold making it the most popular British car ever made.

AUG

31st | Prime minister Harold Macmillan and U.S. president Dwight Eisenhower give an historic live television broadcast from Downing Street. Among the subjects the two leaders discuss are world peace and global poverty. It was the first time that such a broadcast had ever been made and initial protests by the Labour party - fearing the event would jeopardise its chances in the forthcoming General Election - were withdrawn.

SEP

18th | Forty-seven miners die as the result of an underground fire at Auchengeich Colliery, Lanarkshire, Scotland. It is the worst mining disaster in Scottish history and leaves 41 women widowed and 76 children without fathers.

OCT

7th | Three-hundred people need to be rescued when a fire breaks out on Southend Pier. The visitors became stranded when a large wooden pavilion at the shore end of the pier caught fire in the early evening and caused £100,000 in damage; the pier is a major landmark in Southend-on-Sea, extending 1.34-miles into the Thames Estuary, and is the longest pleasure pier in the world.

8th | Harold Macmillan and the Conservative Party increase their majority to 100 seats in the General Election. It is the Conservatives third successive victory and sees a 33 year old Margaret Thatcher, representing Finchley in North London, among its new members of parliament.

30th | Saxophonist Ronnie Scott opens a jazz club in a basement in London's Soho with fellow saxophonist and friend Pete King. Many prestigious artists would play there over the coming years including Earl 'Fatha' Hines, Chet Baker, Ella Fitzgerald, Anita O'Day, Nina Simone, Jimi Hendrix, George Benson and Prince.

NOV

2nd | The first section of the M1 motorway is opened between Watford and Rugby.

5th | Philip John Noel-Baker wins the Nobel Peace Prize as a 'lifelong ardent worker for international peace and co-operation'. Noel-Baker, a talented amateur athlete, is notably the only person to have won an Olympic medal (1500m Silver in 1920) as well as receive a Nobel Prize.

14th | The nuclear Dounreay Fast Reactor in Scotland achieves criticality.

17th | Prestwick and Renfrew airports become the first in the UK to have duty-free shops.

DEC

| | Russian-born British engineer and health enthusiast Dr. Barbara Moore walks from Edinburgh to London. Dr. Moore demonstrated her theories about dieting and exercise with lengthy treks in Europe and the United States, and in July 1960 became the first woman to complete the 3,387-mile marathon walk from San Francisco to New York.

7th | The Aberdeen trawler George Robb runs aground at Duncansby Head in Scotland with the loss of all 12 crew.

8th | The Broughty Ferry life-boat RNLB Mona capsizes on service to North Carr Lightship in Scotland: all eight lifeboat crew are lost.

28th | Associated-Rediffusion first airs the children's television series Ivor the Engine, made by Oliver Postgate and Peter Firmin's Smallfilms. The series was originally made for black and white television but was revived in 1975 when new episodes in colour were produced for the BBC.

1959 - Undated

The iconic British made Bush TR82 transistor radio, by Ogle Design, is launched.

British Publications First Printed In 1959

- Agatha Christie's novel Cat Among The Pigeons.
- Ian Fleming's novel Goldfinger.
- Colin MacInnes' novel Absolute Beginners.
- Spike Milligan's collection Silly Verse For Kids.
- Iona and Peter Opie's study The Lore And Language Of Schoolchildren.
- Mervyn Peake's novel Titus Alone, the last of the Gormenghast series.
- Alan Sillitoe's story The Loneliness Of The Long Distance Runner.
- Keith Waterhouse's novel Billy Liar.

Notable British Deaths

22nd Jan	John Michael Hawthorn (b. 10th April 1929) - Racing driver who became the United Kingdom's first Formula One World Champion driver in 1958.
15th Feb	Sir Owen Willans Richardson, FRS (b. 26th April 1879) - Recipient of the Nobel Prize in Physics in 1928 for "his work on the thermionic phenomenon and especially for the discovery of the law named after him".
21st Feb	Kathleen Freeman (b. 22nd June 1897) - Classical scholar and (under the pseudonym Mary Fitt) author of detective novels, who was a lecturer in Greek at the University College of South Wales and Monmouthshire, Cardiff between 1919 and 1946.
11th Jul	Charles Warrington Leonard 'Charlie' Parker (b. 14th October 1882) - Cricketer who stands as the third highest wicket taker in the history of first-class cricket behind Wilfred Rhodes and Tich Freeman.

5th Aug	Edgar Albert Guest (b. 20th August 1881) - Prolific English-born American poet who became known as the People's Poet.
19th Aug	Sir Jacob Epstein, KBE (b. 10th November 1880) - American-British sculptor who helped pioneer modern sculpture and challenge ideas on what was appropriate subject matter for public artworks.

  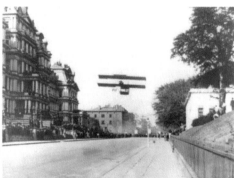

19th August - Claude Grahame-White (b. 21st August 1879) - Pioneer of aviation who was the first pilot to make a night flight during the Daily Mail sponsored 1910 London to Manchester air race. Grahame-White was also one of the first people to qualify as pilot in England, becoming the holder of Royal Aero Club Cert. No.6. One of his many other notable feats was flying his Farman biplane over Washington D.C. in October 1910 and landing next to the White House (top right photo).

6th Sep	Kay Kendall (b. 21st May 1927) - Actress and comedian who won a Golden Globe Award for Best Actress for her role in the musical-comedy film Les Girls (1957).
21st Sep	Agnes Nicholls (b. 14th July 1876) - One of the greatest English sopranos of the 20th century in both the concert hall and on the operatic stage.
25th Sep	Dame Elvira Sibyl Marie Mathews, DBE (b. 25th September 1888) - One of the first officers in the Women's Royal Naval Service (WRNS), serving from just after the inception of the WRNS in 1918 until it was disbanded in late 1919. She later served as Director of the re-founded WRNS from 1939 until 1946.
28th Sep	Gerard Hoffnung (b. 22nd March 1925) - German born artist and musician (brought to London as a boy to escape the Nazis), best known for his humorous works.
15th Nov	Charles Wilson, CH, FRS (b. 14th February 1869) - Physicist and meteorologist who won the Nobel Prize in Physics for his invention of the cloud chamber.
26th Nov	Albert William Ketelbey (b. 9th August 1875) - Composer, conductor and pianist, best known for his short pieces of light orchestral music.
14th Dec	Sir Stanley Spencer, CBE, RA (b. 30th June 1891) - Painter who was one of the leading artists in England between the first and second World Wars.

1. 2nd January - The USSR launches Mechta (Luna 1) which becomes the first craft to leave Earth's gravity on its intended route to impact the Moon. Due to a programming error the duration of the upper stage burn was incorrectly set; Luna 1 missed its target passing within 3,725-miles of the Moon's surface. As a consequence of this it became the first spacecraft to be placed in a heliocentric orbit - today it still remains in orbit around the Sun between Earth and Mars.
2. 8th January - Charles de Gaulle is inaugurated as president of France's 5th Republic.
3. 12th January - American record company Motown is founded by Berry Gordy Jr. as Tamla Records; it was incorporated as Motown Record Corporation a year later on the 14th April 1960.

4. 3rd February - A chartered plane transporting musicians Buddy Holly, Ritchie Valens and The Big Bopper crashes in foggy conditions near Clear Lake, Iowa, killing all 4 occupants on board, including pilot Roger Peterson. The tragedy is later termed 'The Day The Music Died', and was popularised in Don McLean's 1972 song American Pie. *Photos L-R; Buddy Holly, The Big Bopper and Ritchie Valens.*

5. 6th February - At Cape Canaveral, Florida, the first successful test firing of the U.S. Titan intercontinental ballistic missile (ICBM) is accomplished.
6. 16th February - Fidel Castro comes to power in Cuba after overthrowing Fulgencio Batista during the Cuban Revolution.
7. 17th February - The United States Navy launch Vanguard 2 to measure cloud cover and to provide information on the density of the atmosphere. As the world's first weather satellite it is an important part of the space race between the United States and the Soviet Union.
8. 24th March - At the Institute of Radio Engineers' annual trade show at the New York Coliseum in New York City, Texas Instruments, one of the U.S.'s leading electronics firms, introduces the solid integrated circuit (aka the microchip).
9. 31st March - The Dalai Lama, fleeing the Chinese suppression of a national uprising in Tibet, crosses the border into India after an epic 15-day journey on foot over the Himalayan mountains. Once in India he is granted political asylum.
10. 27th April - Mao Zedong resigns as Chairman of the People's Republic of China after the disastrous failure of the Great Leap Forward.
11. 4th May - The 1st Annual Grammy Awards are held to recognise musical accomplishments of performers for the year 1958. Two separate ceremonies were held simultaneously in Beverly Hills and New York City, with Count Basie, Domenico Modugno, Henry Mancini, Ella Fitzgerald and Perry Como amongst the winners.

12. 9th June - The United States submarine USS George Washington (SSBN-598) is launched at Groton, Connecticut, and is the first submarine to carry ballistic missiles (16 Polaris A-1 missiles). The submarine was commissioned on the 30th December 1959.

13. 8th August - Chinese-American reproductive biologist Min Chueh Chang reports the first mammals (a litter of rabbits) grown from ova having undergone in vitro fertilisation and transferred to a surrogate mother.

14. 12th September - Luna 2 is launched by the USSR and becomes the first spacecraft to reach the surface of the Moon, and the first man-made object to land on another celestial body.

15. 20th to 27th September - Typhoon Vera strikes Japan killing at least 4,000 people. It is the deadliest typhoon in Japanese history and causes damage equivalent to around US$5.04 billion today.

16. 19th September - Giuseppe Cocconi and Philip Morrison establish the scientific rationale for SETI with the publishing of their seminal paper 'Searching for Interstellar Communications'.

17. 4th October - The Russian probe Luna 3 sends back the first images of the far side of the Moon. These historic never-before-seen views of the far side of the Moon caused excitement and interest when they were published around the world. They depicted a mountainous terrain with just two dark low-lying regions, very different from the near side of the Moon.

18. 5th October - The IBM 1401, considered to be the Model T Ford of the computer industry because it was mass-produced and because of its sales volume, is announced by IBM. Some 12,000 units would be manufactured during the years that followed, with many leased or resold after they were replaced with newer technology. The 1401 was eventually withdrawn on the 8th February 1971.

19. 22nd to 28th October - The deadliest Pacific hurricane on record kills 1,800 people in Western Mexico.

20. 18th November - MGM's widescreen, multimillion-dollar, Technicolor version of Ben-Hur, starring Charlton Heston, premieres in New York City. It is critically acclaimed and eventually wins 11 Academy Awards; a record which has only ever been equalled by Titanic (1997) and The Lord of the Rings: The Return of the King (2003).

21. 24th November - A 150kg meteorite makes a landfall in Azerbaijan. During its descent it was accompanied by a bright blinding flare which illuminated and area of 1,100 sq mi.

22. 1st December - The Antarctic Treaty is signed in Washington by the twelve countries that had been active in the Antarctic region during the previous year; the United States, United Kingdom, Soviet Union, Norway, Japan, New Zealand, South Africa, Belgium, France, Argentina, Chile, and Australia. The purpose of the treaty was to guarantee peaceful use of the uninhabited continent for scientific purposes and global cooperation. The treaty became effective on the 23rd June 1961 and has since been expanded to include a total of 53 countries.

23. 4th December - Little Joe 2, a mission to test the Mercury space capsule, carries Sam the monkey into space. The flight was launched from Wallops Island, Virginia, U.S. and flew to an altitude of 55 miles. After 11 minutes and 6 seconds it returned to Earth and was then recovered in the Atlantic Ocean by USS Borie.

24. 11th December - Emilio G. Segrè and Owen Chamberlain publish their discovery of the antiproton for which they are both awarded the 1959 Nobel Prize in Physics.

25. Notable releases / inventions from 1959: Mattel release the Barbie Doll, Wilson Greatbatch invents the internal pacemaker, Joseph-Armand Bombardier patents the Ski-Doo snowmobile (originally christened the Ski-Dog, but renamed because of a typographical error that Bombardier decided not to change), and Eveready engineer Lewis Urry invents the long-lasting alkaline battery.

U.K. PERSONALITIES
BORN IN 1959

Helen Folasade Adu,
CBE
16th January 1959

British Nigerian singer and songwriter known professionally as Sade Adu or simply Sade. Backed by members Paul S. Denman, Andrew Hale and Stuart Matthewman, she gained worldwide fame as the lead vocalist of the British band Sade. In 2010, The Sunday Times described Sade as the most successful solo British female artist in history and in 2012, she was listed at No.30 on VH1's '100 Greatest Women In Music'. Sade has sold more than 75 million records worldwide to date.

Steve McFadden
20th March 1959

Actor, born Steve Robert Reid, best known for his role as hardman Phil Mitchell in the BBC soap opera EastEnders (which he has played since 1990). After graduating from RADA in 1987 he made his acting debut playing a small role in the 1988 television film The Firm. That same year he also had an uncredited brief appearance in the film Buster as a gang member. This was subsequently followed by appearances in the television series The Bill, Minder and Bergerac before he started with his role in EastEnders.

Emma Thompson,
DBE
15th April 1959

One of Britain's most acclaimed actresses and a screenwriter who has, as of July 2017, appeared in forty-four films, twenty television programmes and eight stage productions. She has won and been nominated for many awards throughout her career including five Academy Award nominations (winning two), nine Golden Globe Award nominations (winning two), seven BAFTA Award nominations (winning three), and six Emmy Award nominations (winning one).

Peter Doig
17th April 1959

Scottish painter who is one of the most renowned living figurative painters. In 2007 his painting White Canoe sold at Sotheby's for $11.3 million, then an auction record for a living European artist. In 2017 another of his paintings, Rosedale (1991), was sold at auction for $28.8 million to a telephone bidder. Art critic Jonathan Jones said about him: "Amid all the nonsense, impostors, rhetorical bullshit and sheer trash that pass for art in the 21st century, Doig is a jewel of genuine imagination, sincere work and humble creativity."

Shaun Mark Bean
17th April 1959

Actor who first found mainstream success with his portrayal of Richard Sharpe in the ITV series Sharpe. Bean has since garnered further recognition for his performance as Ned Stark in the HBO epic fantasy series Game Of Thrones, as well as roles in the BBC anthology series Accused and the ITV historical drama series Henry VIII. He has received several awards throughout his career and was the winner of an International Emmy for Best Actor for his role in Accused.

Robert James Smith
21st April 1959

Singer, songwriter and musician who is the lead singer, guitarist, multi-instrumentalist, lyricist, principal songwriter and only consistent member of the rock band the Cure (which he co-founded in 1976). He was also the lead guitarist for the band Siouxsie And The Banshees from 1982 to 1984, and was part of the short-lived group The Glove in 1983. Smith is known for his distinctive voice and unique stage look, the latter of which was influential on the Goth subculture that rose to prominence in the 1980s.

Sheena Shirley Easton
27th April 1959

Scottish-American singer, recording artist and stage and screen actress. Easton first came into the public eye as the focus of an episode in the first British musical reality television programme The Big Time: Pop Singer, which recorded her attempts to gain a record contract and her eventual signing with EMI Records. A two-time Grammy Award winner she has recorded 16 studio albums and released 45 singles worldwide, selling over 20 million records in total.

Benjamin Charles Elton
3rd May 1959

British-Australian comedian, author, playwright, actor and director. He was a part of London's alternative comedy movement in the 1980s and became a writer on series such as The Young Ones and Blackadder, as well as continuing as a stand-up comedian on stage and television. Since then he has also published 15 novels and written the musicals We Will Rock You (2002) and Love Never Dies (2010), the sequel to The Phantom Of The Opera.

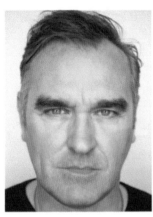

Steven Patrick Morrissey
22nd May 1959

Singer, songwriter and author, known mononymously as Morrissey, who rose to prominence as the frontman of the Smiths (1982-1987). Since then he has had a solo career making the Top 10 of the UK Singles Chart on ten occasions and reaching No.1 on the UK Albums Chart three times. Highly influential, Morrissey has been credited as a seminal figure in the emergence of indie rock and Britpop. In a 2006 poll held by the BBC's The Culture Show, Morrissey was voted the second greatest living British cultural icon behind David Attenborough.

Rupert James Hector Everett
29th May 1959

Actor and writer who first came to public attention in 1981 when he was cast in Julian Mitchell's play and subsequent film Another Country (1984). Everett has since performed in many prominent films, including The Madness Of King George (1994), My Best Friend's Wedding (1997), Shakespeare In Love (1998), Inspector Gadget (1999), An Ideal Husband (1999), The Chronicles of Narnia: The Lion, The Witch And The Wardrobe (2005), the Shrek sequels and Miss Peregrine's Home For Peculiar Children (2016).

Martin John Brundle
1st June 1959

Racing driver best known as a Formula One driver and as a commentator for ITV Sport from 1997 to 2008, the BBC from 2009 to 2011, and Sky Sports from 2012. Brundle contested the 1983 British Formula Three Championship, finishing a close second to Ayrton Senna - the two progressed to Formula One the next year. Brundle failed to win a race in F1 but he did have success in other disciplines; he was the 1988 World Sportscar Champion, with a record points score, and won the 1990 24 Hours of Le Mans race with Jaguar Cars.

James Hugh Calum Laurie, CBE
11th June 1959

Actor, director, musician, comedian, and author. He first gained recognition as one half of the comedy double act Fry And Laurie with Stephen Fry. The duo acted together in a number of projects during the 1980s and 1990s, including the sketch comedy series A Bit Of Fry & Laurie and the P.G. Wodehouse adaptation Jeeves and Wooster. Laurie's other roles have included the comedy series Blackadder, the U.S. medical drama series House and films such as Sense And Sensibility and Stuart Little.

James Kerr
9th July 1959

Singer-songwriter and the lead singer of the rock band Simple Minds. Kerr has achieved five UK No.1 albums with the band and a No.1 single in 1989 with Belfast Child. He released his first solo album, Lostboy! AKA Jim Kerr in 2010 but continues to record and tour with Simple Minds, who released their latest studio album Walk Between Worlds in February 2018. During their career Simple Minds have sold an estimated 60 million albums with Kerr and Charlie Burchill today the bands only remaining founding members.

Simon Phillip Cowell
7th October 1959

Reality television judge and producer. He has judged on the British TV talent competition series Pop Idol, The X Factor, and Britain's Got Talent, and also on the equivalent American productions. He has produced and promoted singles and albums for various singers whom he has taken under his wing and is popularly known for signing successful boybands such as Westlife, One Direction and CNCO. In 2008 The Daily Telegraph ranked him sixth in their list of the '100 most powerful people in British culture'.

Kirsty Anna MacColl
10th October 1959 -
18th December 2000

Singer and songwriter who recorded several pop hits in the 1980s and 1990s, including 'There's A Guy Works Down The Chip Shop Swears He's Elvis' and cover versions of Billy Bragg's 'A New England' and The Kinks' 'Days'. Her song 'They Don't Know' was covered with great success by Tracey Ullman. MacColl also sang on recordings produced by her husband Steve Lillywhite and most notably on the perennial Christmas favourite 'Fairytale Of New York' by The Pogues.

Sarah Margaret Ferguson, Sarah, Duchess of York
15th October 1959

Writer, charity patron, public speaker, film producer and television personality. She is the former wife of Prince Andrew, Duke of York and is the younger daughter of Major Ronald Ferguson and Susan Barrantes (née Wright). Sarah has two daughters, Princesses Beatrice and Eugenie of York, who are respectively 8th and 9th in the line of succession to the throne. Since the divorce Sarah has still attended some functions with her daughters and on those occasions she has still been afforded treatment as a member of the Royal Family.

Gary James Kemp
16th October 1959

Pop musician and actor who is the guitar player and chief songwriter for the 1980s new wave band Spandau Ballet (alongside his brother Martin Kemp who plays bass guitar in the band). Kemp has also provided backing vocals on many of the band's tracks behind lead singer Tony Hadley. Spandau Ballet became one of the most successful groups to emerge during the New Romantic era and at the height of their popularity in 1984 received a Brit Award for technical excellence. The band split in 1990 with the members pursuing solo careers but reformed again in 2009.

Charles Peter Kennedy
25th November 1959 - 1st June 2015

Scottish Liberal Democrat politician who was Leader of the Liberal Democrats from 1999 to 2006 and a Member of Parliament from 1983 to 2015 (latterly for the Ross, Skye and Lochaber constituency). In 1999 after the resignation of Paddy Ashdown, Kennedy was elected as party leader at the age of 39. A charismatic and affable speaker in public, he led the party through two general elections and increased their seats in the House of Commons to their highest level since 1923.

Lorraine Kelly, OBE
30th November 1959

Scottish television presenter, journalist, model and actress. She has presented on TV-am, GMTV, ITV Breakfast, Daybreak and Lorraine. Since 2011 she has also hosted the annual STV Children's Appeal and sister shows such as STV Appeal Stories and Lorraine & Friends. Kelly was appointed an OBE in the 2012 New Year Honours for services to charity and the armed forces, and in 2014 received a special Scottish BAFTA award honouring her 30-year television career.

Eamonn Holmes, OBE
3rd December 1959

Journalist and broadcaster from Northern Ireland best known for presenting Sky News Sunrise and This Morning. He co-presented GMTV for twelve years between 1993 and 2005 before presenting Sky News Sunrise for eleven years between 2005 and 2016. Since 2006 he has co-hosted This Morning with his wife Ruth Langsford on Fridays and during school holidays. Holmes is an advocate of numerous charities and causes including Dogs Trust, Variety GB and Northern Ireland Kidney Patients' Association.

Keith Kelvin Deller
24th December 1959

Former professional darts player who won the Embassy World Professional Darts Championship in 1983. He was the first qualifier ever to win the championship and remains one of its youngest champions. Deller has for many years been part of the Sky Sports broadcasting team acting as a 'spotter' for the cameras helping anticipate where the next dart will be thrown. In 2012 Deller set the World Record of the quickest 301 in a time of 25 seconds.

Steven Billy Mitchell, CBE, DCM, MM
28th December 1959

Novelist and former Special Air Service (SAS) sergeant usually known by the pseudonym and pen-name of Andy McNab. McNab came into public prominence in 1993 when he published his account of the SAS patrol Bravo Two Zero, for which he had been awarded the Distinguished Conduct Medal in 1991. He had previously received the Military Medal for an action while serving with the Royal Green Jackets in Northern Ireland in 1979. In addition to Bravo Two Zero he has written two other autobiographies and a number of fiction books.

Tracey Ullman
30th December 1959

English actress, comedian, singer, dancer, screenwriter, producer, director, author and businesswoman, who holds both British and American citizenship. Her earliest appearances were on the television sketch comedy shows A Kick Up The Eighties and Three Of A Kind. In 1985 she emigrated to the US where she starred in her own network television comedy series. Since then Ullman has been nominated for twenty-four Emmys and is a seven-time winner of the award. In 2009 she was awarded a Lifetime Achievement BAFTA.

1959 TOP 10 SINGLES

Russ Conway	No.1	Side Saddle
Cliff Richard & The Drifters	No.2	Living Doll
Buddy Holly	No.3	It Doesn't Matter Anymore
Bobby Darin	No.4	Dream Lover
Elvis Presley	No.5	A Fool Such As I
The Platters	No.6	Smoke Gets In Your Eyes
Shirley Bassey	No.7	As I Love You
Craig Douglas	No.8	Only Sixteen
Cliff Richard & The Shadows	No.9	Travellin' Light
Bobby Darin	No.10	Mack The Knife

Russ Conway
Side Saddle

Label:	Written by:	Length:
Columbia	Trevor Stanford	1 mins 51 secs

Russ Conway, DSM (b. Trevor Herbert Stanford; 2nd September 1925 - d. 16th November 2000) was a popular music pianist and composer. Before his musical career he served in the Royal Navy during WW2 earning the distinguished service medal for 'gallantry and devotion to duty'. Conway went on to have 20 piano instrumentals in the UK Singles Chart between 1957 and 1963, including this, his biggest hit, Side Saddle. In total throughout his career Conway sold over 30m records.

Cliff Richard & The Drifters
Living Doll

Label:	Written by:	Length:
Columbia	Lionel Bart	2 mins 31 secs

Sir Cliff Richard, OBE (b. Harry Rodger Webb; 14th October 1940) is a pop singer, musician, performer, actor and philanthropist. He has total sales of over 21 million singles in the UK and is the third-top-selling artist in UK Singles Chart history (behind the Beatles and Elvis Presley). Living Doll was his fifth record and became his first No.1 hit. By this time in 1959 the original Drifters line-up had changed with the arrival of Jet Harris, Tony Meehan, Hank Marvin and Bruce Welch.

③ Buddy Holly
It Doesn't Matter Anymore

Label:
Coral

Written by:
Paul Anka

Length:
2 mins 1 sec

Charles Hardin Holley (b. 7th September 1936 - d. 3rd February 1959), more popularly known as just Buddy Holly, was a musician, singer-songwriter and record producer who was a central and pioneering figure of mid-1950s rock and roll. During his short career Holly wrote, recorded, and produced his own material. He is often regarded as the artist who defined the traditional rock-and-roll line-up of two guitars, bass, and drums. He was among the first artists inducted into the Rock and Roll Hall of Fame in 1986.

---

④ Bobby Darin
Dream Lover

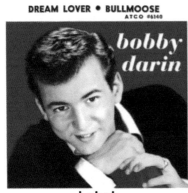

Label:
London Records

Written by:
Bobby Darin

Length:
2 mins 28 secs

Bobby Darin (b. Walden Robert Cassotto; 14th May 1936 - d. 20th December 1973) was an American singer, songwriter, multi-instrumentalist, and actor in film and television. He performed jazz, pop, rock and roll, folk, swing, and country music. He started his career as a songwriter for Connie Francis and recorded his first million-selling single 'Splish Splash' in 1958. This was followed by Dream Lover which reached the No.1 spot in the UK for four weeks during June and July 1959, and featured Neil Sedaka on piano.

⑤ Elvis Presley
A Fool Such As I

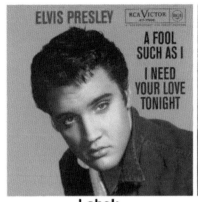  

Label:	**Written by:**	**Length:**
RCA Victor	Bill Trader	2 mins 36 secs

Elvis Aaron Presley (b. 8th January 1935 - d. 16th August 1977) was an American singer and actor. Regarded as one of the most significant cultural icons and influential musicians of the 20th century, he is often referred to as 'the King of Rock and Roll', or simply, 'the King'. Commercially successful in many genres, including pop, blues and gospel, he is the best-selling solo artist in the history of recorded music with estimated record sales of around 600 million units worldwide. He won three Grammys and also received the Grammy Lifetime Achievement Award at the age of 36.

⑥ The Platters
Smoke Gets In Your Eyes

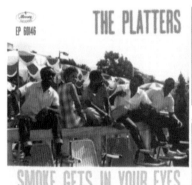 

Label:	**Written by:**	**Length:**
Mercury	Harbach / Kern	2 mins 36 secs

The Platters are one of the most successful vocal groups of the early rock and roll era. They have been through several personnel changes over the years but the most successful incarnation comprised of Tony Williams, David Lynch, Paul Robi, Herb Reed, and Zola Taylor. The group had 40 charting singles on the U.S. Billboard Hot 100 chart between 1955 and 1967, including four No.1 hits, and were for a period of time the most successful vocal group in the world.

⑦ Shirley Bassey
As I Love You

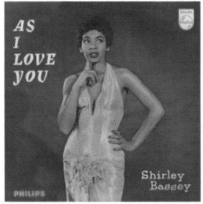

Label:	Written by:	Length:
Philips	Livingston / Evans	2 mins 18 secs

Dame Shirley Veronica Bassey, DBE (b. 8th January 1937) is a Welsh singer whose career began in the mid-1950s and is best known both for her powerful voice and for recording the theme songs to the James Bond films Goldfinger (1964), Diamonds Are Forever (1971), and Moonraker (1979). Bassey has been called 'one of the most popular female vocalists in Britain during the last half of the 20th century'. In January 1959, 'As I Love You' reached No.1 and stayed there for four weeks; it was the first ever No.1 single by a Welsh artist.

⑧ Craig Douglas
Only Sixteen

Label:	Written by:	Length:
Top Rank International	Sam Cooke	2 mins 15 secs

Craig Douglas (b. Terence Perkins; 12th August 1941) is a pop singer who was popular in the late 1950s and early 1960s. He was voted 'Best New Singer' in 1959 by the British music magazine NME and went on to record a total of 9 Top 40 UK singles (eight of which were cover versions of former American hit songs). Only Sixteen was his sole UK chart-topper which, in the UK, out-sold Sam Cooke's original version.

⑨ Cliff Richard & The Shadows
Travellin' Light

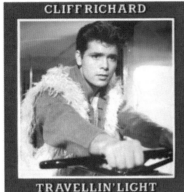

Label:	Written by:	Length:
Columbia	Tepper / Bennett	2 mins 36 secs

Travellin' Light was the first recording naming The Shadows as Cliff Richard's backing band. The band, formerly called the Drifters, was obliged to change their name after legal complications with the American group of the same name. Travellin' Light was the follow-up single to Richard's first No.1, Living Doll, and it too made it to the No.1 spot where it stayed for 5 weeks. The B-side, 'Dynamite', also made the UK Charts and peaked at No.16.

---

⑩ Bobby Darin
Mack The Knife

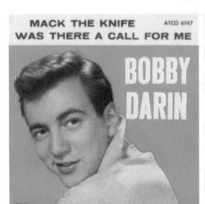

Label:	Written by:	Length:
London Records	Brecht / Weill	3 mins 4 secs

Mack The Knife, originally called 'Die Moritat von Mackie Messer', was a song composed by Kurt Weill with lyrics by Bertolt Brecht for their music drama Die Dreigroschenoper, or, as it is known in English, The Threepenny Opera. It premiered in Berlin in 1928 and the song has since become a popular standard recorded by many artists. This 1959 US and UK No.1 hit earned Darin a Grammy Award for Record Of The Year.

1959: TOP FILMS

1. **Ben-Hur** - *MGM*
2. **Operation Petticoat** - *Universal Pictures*
3. **Some Like It Hot** - *United Artists*
4. **The Shaggy Dog** - *Disney*
5. **Pillow Talk** - *Universal Pictures*

OSCARS

Best Picture: Ben-Hur

Best Director: William Wyler *(Ben-Hur)*

Best Actor:
Charlton Heston *(Ben-Hur)*

Best Actress:
Simone Signoret *(Room At The Top)*

Best Supporting Actor:
Hugh Griffith *(Ben-Hur)*

Best Supporting Actress:
Shelley Winters *(The Diary Of Anne Frank)*

BEN-HUR

Directed by: William Wyler - Runtime: 3 hours 32 minutes

A rich Jewish prince called Judah Ben-Hur is betrayed and sent into slavery by his old childhood friend Messala, the new Roman governor of Jerusalem. Judah regains his freedom and seeks revenge against his one-time friend.

STARRING

Charlton Heston
Born: 4th October 1923
Died: 5th April 2008

Character:
Judah Ben-Hur

Born John Charles Carter, Heston was an actor and political activist. As a Hollywood star he appeared in around 100 films over the course of 60 years. For his role as Moses in The Ten Commandments (1956) he received his first Golden Globe Award nomination and in 1959 won the Academy Award for Best Actor playing the titular character in Ben-Hur. Other notable films include El Cid (1961) and Planet Of The Apes (1968).

Jack Hawkins, CBE
Born: 14th September 1910
Died: 18th July 1973

Character:
Quintus Arrius

Actor who worked on stage and in film. He made his London stage debut aged eleven playing the Elf King in Where The Rainbow Ends (December 1923). Hawkins was one of the most popular British film stars of the 1950s and was best known for his portrayal of military men in films like, Angels One Five (1951), The Cruel Sea (1953), Bridge On The River Kwai (1957), Ben-Hur and Lawrence Of Arabia (1962).

Haya Harareet
Born: 20th September 1931

Character:
Esther

Israeli actress who is perhaps best known for playing Esther, Charlton Heston's love interest in Ben-Hur. Harareet began her career in Israeli films with Hill 24 Doesn't Answer (1955), which was nominated for the Palme d'Or at the 1955 Cannes Film Festival. During her career she appeared in just a handful of other films including The Doll That Took The Town (1957), L'Atlantide (1961), The Secret Partner (1961) and The Interns (1962).

TRIVIA

Goofs | Sheik Ilderim pins a Star of David onto Ben-Hur's belt before the chariot race, presumably in an attempt to goad the Romans. The Star of David didn't become a symbol of Judaism until the Middle Ages in Eastern Europe.

When Judah and Messala argue in the courtyard of Judah's home, road noise and honking horns from cars can be heard in the background. For some reason these were not removed from the soundtrack post production.

During the chariot race a Volkswagen Beetle can be seen in the background.

CONTINUED

Interesting Facts

Ben-Hur is the first of three films to have won 11 Academy Awards; the second was Titanic (1997) and the third was The Lord of the Rings: The Return of the King (2003).

The chariot race required 15,000 extras on a set constructed on 18 acres of backlot at Cinecitta Studios outside Rome. Eighteen chariots were built, with half being used for practice. The race took five weeks to film.

Martha Scott was 45 years old at the time of filming, only ten years older than her screen son Charlton Heston. Three years previously she also played Heston's mother in The Ten Commandments (1956).

Paul Newman was offered the role of Judah Ben-Hur but turned it down because he'd already done one Biblical-era film, The Silver Chalice (1954), and hated the experience. He also said it taught him that he didn't have the legs to wear a tunic.

During an 18-day auction of MGM props, costumes and memorabilia in May 1970, a Sacramento restaurateur paid $4,000 for a chariot used in the film. Three years later, during the energy crisis, he was arrested for driving the chariot on the highway.

Ben-Hur is the only Hollywood film to make the Vatican approved film list in the category of religion.

Quote

Sextus: You can break a man's skull, you can arrest him, you can throw him into a dungeon. But how do you control what's up here?
[taps his head]
Sextus: How do you fight an idea?

OPERATION PETTICOAT

CARY GRANT · TONY CURTIS

OPERATION PETTICOAT

in Eastman COLOR

Co-starring
JOAN O'BRIEN · DINA MERRILL · GENE EVANS with DICK SARGENT
and ARTHUR O'CONNELL

Directed by: Blake Edwards - Runtime: 2 hours 4 minutes

During World War II a commander finds himself stuck with a decrepit (pink) submarine, a staff officer with no discernible naval experience and a group of army nurses.

STARRING

Cary Grant
Born: 18th January 1904
Died: 29th November 1986

Character:
Lt. Cmdr. Matt T. Sherman

British-American actor known as one of classic Hollywood's definitive leading men. He began a career in Hollywood in the early 1930s and became known for his transatlantic accent, light-hearted approach to acting, comic timing and debonair demeanour. He was twice nominated for the Academy Award for Best Actor for his roles in Penny Serenade (1941) and None But The Lonely Heart (1944); in 1970 he was given an Honorary Oscar for Lifetime Achievement.

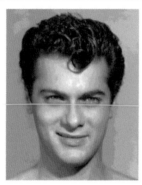

Tony Curtis
Born: 3rd June 1925
Died: 29th September 2010

Character:
Lt. JG Nicholas Holden

Actor born Bernard Schwartz whose career spanned six decades. He appeared in more than 100 films throughout his career, in roles covering a wide range of genres from light comedy to serious drama. Curtis was nominated for an Oscar for Best Actor in The Defiant Ones (1958) and starred in many other notable film roles including Some Like It Hot (1959), Operation Petticoat, Spartacus (1960), and The Boston Strangler (1968).

Joan O'Brien
Born: 14th February 1936

Character:
Lt. Dolores Crandall RN

Actress and singer who made a name for herself acting in television shows in the 1950s and 1960s. Her career began in 1949 when her singing abilities came to the attention of Cliffie Stone, who hired her as a regular performer on his television show Hometown Jamboree. O'Brien had a short film career (1958-1964) but during that time she co-starred with Cary Grant, Elvis Presley, John Wayne and Jerry Lewis. She retired from acting altogether in 1965.

TRIVIA

Goofs	The map on the office wall, where Cary Grant and his superior are discussing the damages to the submarine, is clearly a mid '50s world map. The borders of European countries are clearly post war and it shows both India and Pakistan; they didn't exist as separate countries until 1947.
	When the station wagon crashes into the limousine the sound of the crash comes before the actual collision.
Interesting Facts	This was the second time Cary Grant played a submarine commander. The first was Destination Tokyo (1943).

CONTINUED

Interesting Facts

The sinking of the truck in the movie was inspired by real incident that happened in 1944. On the 9th August 1944, USS Bowfin (SS-287) followed four ships into Minami Daito Harbour. As she fired her six bow torpedoes at the moored ships, hitting three and sinking two of them, one torpedo went astray and hit a pier. A bus parked on it was blown up and thrown into the water by the explosion.

Bob Hope always said it was his biggest regret that he turned down this movie.

Tina Louise was offered but turned down the role of Nurse Crandall (eventually played by Joan O'Brien) because Louise didn't like the abundant boob jokes directed at the character.

Quotes

Lt. Cmdr. Matt T. Sherman: When a girl is under 21, she's protected by law. When she's over 65, she's protected by nature. Anywhere in between, she's fair game. Look out.

Lt. Cmdr Matt T. Serman: Sir, Sea Tiger was built to fight. She deserves a better epitaph than 'Commissioned 1940, sunk 1941, engagements none, shots fired none.' Now, you can't let it go that way. That's like a beautiful woman dying an old maid, if you know what I mean by old maid.
Capt. J.B. Henderson: Did you ever sell used cars?
Lt. Cmdr. Matt T.Sherman: No, Sir.
Capt. J.B. Henderson: I've got a hunch you missed your calling.

SOME LIKE IT HOT

Directed by: Billy Wilder - Runtime: 2 hours 1 minute

When two male musicians witness a mob hit they flee the state in an all-female band disguised as women, but further complications set in.

STARRING

Marilyn Monroe
Born: 1st June 1926
Died: 5th August 1962

Character:
Sugar Kane Kowalczyk

Actress, model and singer born Norma Jeane Mortenson. Famous for playing comic 'blonde bombshell' characters, she became one of the most popular sex symbols of the 1950s and was emblematic of the era's attitudes towards sexuality. Although she was a top-billed actress for only a decade her films grossed $200 million by the time of her death in 1962. More than half a century later she continues to be a major popular cultural icon.

Tony Curtis
Born: 3rd June 1925
Died: 29th September 2010

Characters:
Joe / Josephine

Actor born Bernard Schwartz whose career spanned six decades. He appeared in more than 100 films throughout his career, in roles covering a wide range of genres from light comedy to serious drama. Curtis was nominated for an Oscar for Best Actor in The Defiant Ones (1958) and starred in many other notable film roles including Some Like It Hot, Operation Petticoat (1959), Spartacus (1960), and The Boston Strangler (1968).

Jack Lemmon
Born: 8th February 1925
Died: 27th June 2001

Character:
Jerry / Daphne

Actor and musician who starred in over 60 films during his career. He was nominated eight times for an Academy Award, winning twice for his roles in Mister Roberts (1955) and Save The Tiger (1973). Lemmon worked with many of the top actresses of the day including Marilyn Monroe, Natalie Wood, Betty Grable, Janet Leigh, Shirley MacLaine, Doris Day, Rita Hayworth, Ann-Margret and Sophia Loren.

TRIVIA

Goofs	As the band members are organising the party in Daphne's berth, the girl bringing the cheese and crackers is holding a jar of Cheez Whiz. The film is set in 1929, and Cheez Whiz was not introduced to the market until around 1952.
	As Sweet Sue addresses the ballroom audience we hear strings only, yet the brass section behind her is playing.
Interesting Facts	Upon the film's original release the U.S. state of Kansas banned it from being shown because they believed people from Kansas would find cross-dressing 'too disturbing'.

Interesting Facts

Jerry Lewis was offered the role of Jerry/Daphne but declined because he didn't want to dress in drag. When Jack Lemmon received an Oscar nomination for the role Lewis claims Lemmon sent him chocolates every year to thank him.

Marilyn Monroe required 47 takes to get "It's me, Sugar" correct, instead saying either "Sugar, it's me" or "It's Sugar, me". After take 30, Billy Wilder had the line written on a blackboard. Another scene required Monroe to rummage through some drawers and say "Where's the bourbon?" After 40 takes of her saying "Where's the whiskey?", 'Where's the bottle?', or "Where's the bonbon?", Wilder pasted the correct line in one of the drawers. After Monroe became confused about which drawer contained the line, Wilder had it pasted in every drawer. Fifty-nine takes were required for this scene and when she finally does say it, she has her back to the camera, leading some to wonder if Wilder finally gave up and had it dubbed.

A male cabaret dancer named Babette tried to teach Tony Curtis and Jack Lemmon to walk in heels. After about a week Lemmon declined his help saying he didn't want to walk like a woman, but as a man trying to walk like a woman.

Supposedly when Orry-Kelly was measuring all three stars for dresses, he half-jokingly told Marilyn Monroe, "Tony Curtis has a nicer butt than you," at which point Monroe pulled open her blouse and said, "Yeah, but he doesn't have tits like these!"

Quotes

Jerry: Have I got things to tell you!
Joe: What happened?
Jerry: I'm engaged.
Joe: Congratulations. Who's the lucky girl?
Jerry: I am!

Sugar: Real diamonds! They must be worth their weight in gold!

Sugar: Oh, Daphne, how can I ever repay you?
Jerry: Oh, I can think of a million things.
[Sugar gets into bed with him]
Jerry: And that's one of them!

THE SHAGGY DOG

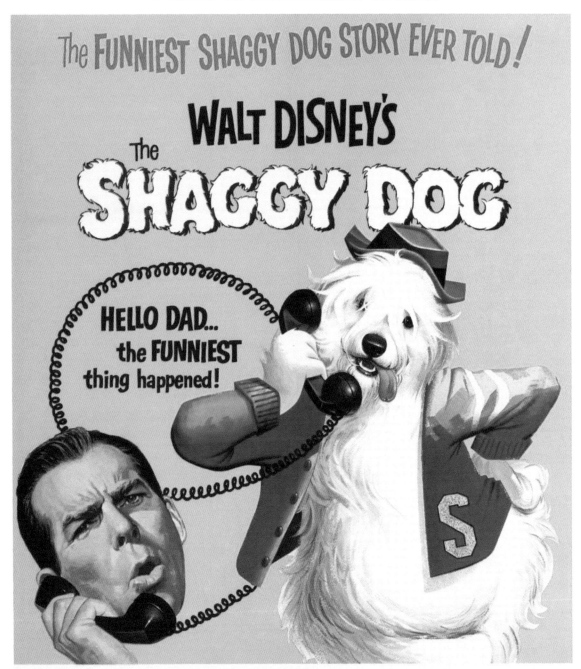

Directed by: Charles Barton - Runtime: 1 hour 44 minutes

An ancient spell causes a boy to keep transforming into a sheepdog at the most inopportune times. It appears that the spell can only be broken through a heroic act of selflessness...

STARRING

Fred MacMurray
Born: 30th August 1908
Died: 5th November 1991

Character:
Wilson Daniels

Actor who appeared in more than 100 films during a career that spanned nearly half a century. MacMurray is best known for his roles in the film Double Indemnity (1944) and for his performances in numerous Disney films including The Shaggy Dog, The Absent-Minded Professor (1961) and The Happiest Millionaire (1967). In 1960 he took the role of Steve Douglas, the widowed patriarch on My Three Sons, which ran on ABC and CBS in the U.S. until 1972.

Jean Hagen
Born: 3rd August 1923
Died: 29th August 1977

Character:
Freeda Daniels

Actress, born Jean Shirley Verhagen, who began her show business career on radio in the 1940s. She is best known for her role as Lina Lamont in Singin' In The Rain (1952) for which she was nominated for an Academy Award for Best Supporting Actress. Hagen was also nominated three times for an Emmy Award for Best Supporting Actress in a Comedy Series for her role as Margaret Williams on the U.S. television series Make Room For Daddy (1953-1956).

Tommy Kirk
Born: 10th December 1941

Character:
Wilby Daniels

A former actor and later a businessman. He is best known for his performances in a number of highly popular movies made by Walt Disney Studios such as, Old Yeller (1957), The Shaggy Dog, The Swiss Family Robinson (1960) and The Misadventures Of Merlin Jones (1964), as well as beach-party movies of the mid-1960s. Kirk was inducted as a Disney Legend for his work in film and television on the 9th October 2006.

TRIVIA

Goofs	In the scene where the boys launch the missile interceptor, the dining room's furnishings (the vase and cabinet behind Fred MacMurray) start to shake before the rocket is even ignited.
	Immediately after Franceska cleans the cut above Buzz Miller's eye the cut disappears.
Interesting Facts	The words Wilby Daniels recites from the ring to turn himself in to a shaggy dog are 'in canis corpore transmuto' (latin for 'I transmute into the body of a dog').

CONTINUED

Interesting Facts

This was the first live-action feature comedy produced by Walt Disney.

As a kind of product placement for Walt Disney's associate publisher Dell, a character is seen reading an Uncle Scrooge comic dated June 1957. This issue (No.18) features the Carl Barks-written adventure 'Land Of The Pygmy Indians'.

Gregory Peck was the second choice for the role of Wilson Daniels.

Although she gets billing above Tim Considine and Roberta Shore, Annette Funicello (in her film debut) has a much smaller role than they do.

This was the first of six Walt Disney films starring Fred MacMurray.

Quotes

Wilby Daniels: What about the seven bucks I loaned you?
Buzz Miller: What about it?
Wilby Daniels: Cough it up. Pop pulled the plug on my allowance.
Buzz Miller: Gee, pal, I'd like to help you out, but you know how it is. I've got a date with Allison.
Wilby Daniels: I'm sick and tired of financing your romances.

Moochie Daniels: Gee, Wilby, you know I like you much better as a dog.

PILLOW TALK

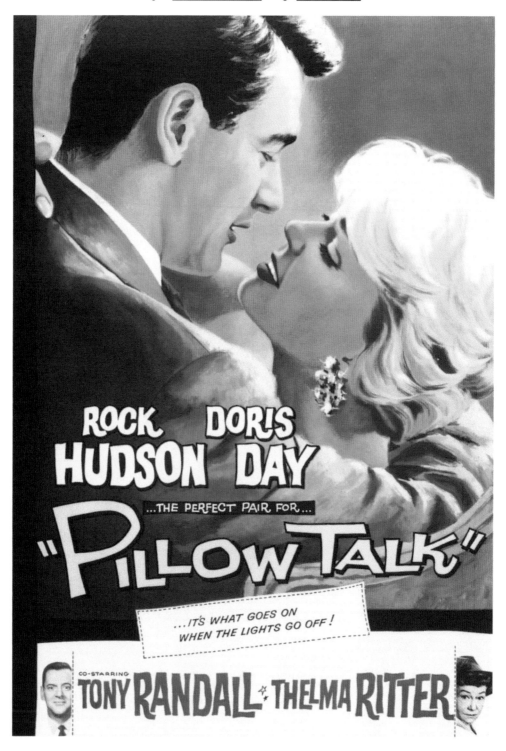

ROCK DORIS
HUDSON DAY
...THE PERFECT PAIR FOR...
"PILLOW TALK"

...IT'S WHAT GOES ON
WHEN THE LIGHTS GO OFF!

CO-STARRING
TONY RANDALL ✴ THELMA RITTER

Directed by: Michael Gordon - Runtime: 1 hour 42 minutes

Playboy songwriter Brad Allen's succession of romances annoys his neighbour, interior designer Jan Morrow, who shares a telephone party line with him and hears all his breezy routines. After Jan unsuccessfully lodges a complaint against him, Brad sets about to seduce her in the guise of an upstanding Texas rancher.

STARRING

Rock Hudson
Born: 17th November 1925
Died: 2nd October 1985

Character:
Brad Allen

Actor and heartthrob generally known for his roles as a leading man in films during the 1950s and 1960s. He first achieved stardom in films such as Magnificent Obsession (1954), All That Heaven Allows (1955) and Giant (1956). Hudson later found continued success with a string of romantic comedies co-starring Doris Day. In total he starred in nearly 70 films and several television productions during a career that spanned over four decades.

Doris Day
Born: 3rd April 1922

Character:
Jan Morrow

An actress, singer, and animal welfare activist born Doris Mary Ann Kappelhoff. After she began her career as a big band singer in 1939 her popularity increased with her first hit recording, Sentimental Journey (1945). She recorded more than 650 songs from 1947 to 1967, becoming one of the most popular and acclaimed singers of the 20th century. Day's film career began with Romance On The High Seas (1948) and its success sparked a 20 year career as a motion picture actress.

Tony Randall
Born: 26th February 1920
Died: 17th May 2004

Characters:
Jonathan Forbes

Actor, born Aryeh Leonard Rosenberg, who is best known for his role as Felix Unger in a television adaptation of the 1965 play The Odd Couple by Neil Simon. In a career spanning around 6 decades, Randall received 6 Golden Globe Award nominations and 6 Primetime Emmy Award nominations (winning one in 1975 for his work on the sitcom The Odd Couple). In 1991, Randall founded the National Actors Theatre at Pace University in New York City.

TRIVIA

Goofs	When Jan and Jonathan are talking in front of the interior design shop about the car he is offering her, the same extras are seen multiple times. A woman with a blue coat and grey hat walks by 4 times, and a woman with a red coat walks by at least 3 times.
	When Brad sees his re-decorated apartment, the cat continues to meow even though its mouth is closed.
Interesting Facts	Doris Day acknowledged that this movie transformed her image from 'the girl next door' to classy sophisticated sex symbol, as the plot for its time was quite racy.

CONTINUED

Interesting Facts

This movie would be the first of three to showcase the trio of Doris Day, Rock Hudson and Tony Randall all together; it was followed by Lover Come Back (1961) and Send Me No Flowers (1964).

Rock Hudson turned down the film three times believing the script to be too risqué. Doris Day finally talked him into starring in it and it subsequently became one of his biggest hits.

Pillow Talk earned Doris Day her only Oscar nomination.

Spanish TV screened Pillow Talk on the 20th July 1969, while everybody was waiting for the Apollo moon landing - it was then stopped suddenly so Spanish people could watch the landing live. The film was not reshown again until 1999, when Spanish viewers could, at last, see the ending.

Quotes

Jan: Officer, arrest this man - he's taking me up to his apartment!
Police Officer: Well, I can't say that I blame him, miss.

Jonathan Forbes: Brad, she is the sweetest, she is the loveliest, she is the most talented woman I have ever met.
Brad Allen: That's what you said when you married that stripper.
Jonathan Forbes: She wasn't a stripper. She was an exotic dancer... with trained doves.

SPORTING WINNERS

BBC SPORTS PERSONALITY OF THE YEAR

JOHN SURTEES - MOTORCYCLE RACING

John Surtees, CBE (b. 11th February 1934 - d. 10th March 2017) was an English Grand Prix motorcycle road racer and Formula One driver. Surtees remains the only person to have been a World Champion on both two and four wheels.

1959	BBC Sports Personality Results	Country	Sport
Winner	**John Surtees**	**England**	**Motorcycle Racing**
Runner Up	Bobby Charlton	England	Football
Third Place	Ian Black	Scotland	Swimming

Motor Racing Statistics:

Competition	1st Place
350cc World Championships	1958, 1959, 1960
500cc World Championships	1956, 1958, 1959, 1960
Formula One	1964

Surtees was inducted into the International Motorsports Hall of Fame in 1996 and in 2003 was honoured by them as a Grand Prix Legend. He was also awarded the 2012 Segrave Trophy in recognition of his multiple world championships.

FIVE NATIONS RUGBY
FRANCE

Position	Nation	Played	Won	Draw	Lost	For	Against	+/-	Points
1	**France**	**4**	**2**	**1**	**1**	**28**	**15**	**+13**	**5**
2	Ireland	4	2	0	2	23	19	+4	4
3	Wales	4	2	0	2	21	23	-2	4
4	England	4	1	2	1	9	11	-2	4
5	Scotland	4	1	1	2	12	25	-13	3

The 1959 Five Nations Championship was the thirtieth series of the rugby union Five Nations Championship. Including the previous incarnations as the Home Nations and Five Nations, this was the sixty-fifth series of the northern hemisphere rugby union championship. Ten matches were played between the 10th January and 18th April, with France winning for the first time in its own right after two shared wins in 1954 and 1955.

Date	Team		Score		Team	Location
10-01-1959	France		9-0		Scotland	Stade Olympique, Paris
17-01-1959	Wales		5-0		England	National Stadium, Cardiff
07-02-1959	Scotland		6-5		Wales	Murrayfield, Edinburgh
14-02-1959	Ireland		0-3		England	Lansdowne Road, Dublin
28-02-1959	England		3-3		France	Twickenham, London
28-02-1959	Scotland		3-8		Ireland	Murrayfield, Edinburgh
14-03-1959	Wales		8-6		Ireland	National Stadium, Cardiff
21-03-1959	England		3-3		Scotland	Twickenham, London
04-04-1959	France		11-3		Wales	Stade Olympique, Paris
18-04-1959	Ireland		9-5		France	Lansdowne Road, Dublin

CALCUTTA CUP

ENGLAND  3-3 SCOTLAND

The Calcutta Cup was first awarded in 1879 and is the rugby union trophy awarded to the winner of the match (currently played as part of the Six Nations Championship) between England and Scotland. The Cup was presented to the Rugby Football Union after the Calcutta Football Club in India disbanded in 1878. It is made from melted down silver rupees withdrawn from the clubs funds.

Historical Records	England	Scotland	Draws
	70 Wins	40 Wins	15

BRITISH GRAND PRIX - JACK BRABHAM

Jack Brabham takes the chequered flag in his Cooper-Climax to win the British Grand Prix.

The 1959 British Grand Prix was held at the Aintree Motor Racing Circuit, Merseyside on the 18th July. The race was won by Australian Jack Brabham, from pole position, driving a works Cooper T51 over 75 laps of the 3 mile circuit. The fastest lap of 1m 57.0s went to Britain's Stirling Moss driving a BRM P25.

Pos.	Country	Driver	Constructor
1	**Australia**	**Jack Brabham**	**Cooper-Climax**
2	United Kingdom	Stirling Moss	BRM
3	New Zealand	Bruce McLaren	Cooper-Climax

1959 GRAND PRIX SEASON

Date	Race	Winning Driver	Constructor
10th May	Monaco Grand Prix	Jack Brabham	Cooper-Climax
30th May	Indianapolis 500	Rodger Ward	Watson-Offenhauser
31st May	Dutch Grand Prix	Joakim Bonnier	BRM
5th Jul	French Grand Prix	Tony Brooks	Ferrari
18th Jul	British Grand Prix	Jack Brabham	Cooper-Climax
2nd Aug	German Grand Prix	Tony Brooks	Ferrari
23rd Aug	Portuguese Grand Prix	Stirling Moss	Cooper-Climax
13th Sep	Italian Grand Prix	Stirling Moss	Cooper-Climax
12th Dec	U.S. Grand Prix	Bruce McLaren	Cooper-Climax

The 1959 Formula One season was the 13th season of FIA Formula One motor racing. It was contested concurrently over a nine race series commencing on the 10th May and ending on the 12th December. Jack Brabham won the World Championship of Drivers in a sport still reeling from the death of several drivers, including reigning champion Mike Hawthorn. The International Cup for F1 Manufacturers was awarded to Cooper-Climax.

GRAND NATIONAL - OXO

The 1959 Grand National was the 113th renewal of this world famous horse race and took place at Aintree Racecourse near Liverpool on the 21st March. The race was won by the 8-1 second-favourite Oxo in a time of 9m 37.2s. Oxo was ridden by Michael Scudamore and trained by Willie Stephenson.

Thirty-four horses contested the 1959 Grand National of which only 4 horses completed the course; 19 fell, 5 were brought down, 3 refused and 3 were pulled up.

Pos.	Name	Jockey	Age	Weight	Odds
1st	**Oxo**	**Michael Scudamore**	**8**	**10st-13lb**	**8-1**
2nd	Wyndburgh	Tim Brookshaw	9	10st-12lb	10-1
3rd	Mr. What	Tosse Taaffe	9	11st-9lb	6-1
4th	Tiberetta	Alan Oughton	11	10st-9lb	20-1

GOLF OPEN CHAMPIONSHIP - GARY PLAYER

South African golfer Gary Player holding the Claret Jug after winning the Open at Muirfield.

The 1959 Open Championship was the 88th to be played and was held between the 1st and 3rd of July at Muirfield Golf Links in Gullane, East Lothian, Scotland. Gary Player, aged 23, shot a final round of 68 to win the first of his nine major titles, two strokes ahead of runners-up Fred Bullock and Flory Van Donck. Player took home £1000 in prize money and the first of his three Claret Jugs; he won again in 1968 and 1974.

FOOTBALL LEAGUE CHAMPIONS

England:

Pos.	Team	W	D	L	F	A	Pts.
1	**Wolverhampton Wanderers**	**28**	**5**	**9**	**110**	**49**	**61**
2	Manchester United	24	7	11	103	66	55
3	Arsenal	21	8	13	88	68	50
4	Bolton Wanderers	20	10	12	79	66	50
5	West Bromwich Albion	18	13	11	88	68	49

Scotland:

Pos.	Team	W	D	L	F	A	Pts.
1	**Rangers**	**21**	**8**	**5**	**92**	**51**	**50**
2	Heart of Midlothian	21	6	7	92	51	48
3	Motherwell	18	8	8	83	50	44
4	Dundee	16	9	9	61	51	41
5	Airdrieonians	15	7	12	64	62	37

FA CUP WINNERS - NOTTINGHAM FOREST

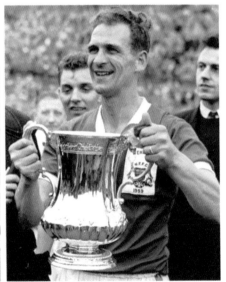

Nottingham Forest captain Jack Burkitt and his team mates celebrate after winning the Cup.

Nottingham Forest   **2-1**   **Luton Town**
Dwight ⚽ 10'   Pacey ⚽ 66'
Wilson ⚽ 14'

The 1959 FA Cup Final took place on the 2nd May at Wembley Stadium in front of 100,000 fans. The game was notable for an unusually large number of stoppages due to injury, particularly when goal-scorer Roy Dwight was carried off the pitch after breaking his leg in a tackle with Brendan McNally after 33 minutes.

WIMBLEDON

Photo 1: Maria Bueno of Brazil holding up the Women's Singles Trophy.
Photo 2: Alex Olmedo receives the Men's Singles Trophy from the Duchess of Kent.

Men's Singles Champion - Alex Olmedo - United States
Ladies Singles Champion - Maria Bueno - Brazil

The 1959 Wimbledon Championships took place on the outdoor grass courts at the All England Lawn Tennis and Croquet Club in Wimbledon, London, and ran from the 22nd June until the 3rd July. It was the 73rd staging of the Wimbledon Championships and the third Grand Slam tennis event of 1959.

Men's Singles Final:

Country	Player	Set 1	Set 2	Set 3
United States	Alex Olmedo	6	6	6
Australia	Rod Laver	4	3	4

Women's Singles Final:

Country	Player	Set 1	Set 2
Brazil	Maria Bueno	6	6
United States	Darlene Hard	4	3

Men's Doubles Final:

Country	Players	Set 1	Set 2	Set 3	Set 4
Australia	Roy Emerson / Neale Fraser	8	6	14	9
Australia	Rod Laver / Bob Mark	6	3	16	7

Women's Doubles Final:

Country	Players	Set 1	Set 2	Set 3
United States	Jeanne Arth / Darlene Hard	2	6	6
United States / United Kingdom	Beverly Fleitz / Christine Truman	6	2	3

Mixed Doubles Final:

Country	Players	Set 1	Set 2
Australia / United States	Rod Laver / Darlene Hard	6	6
Australia / Brazil	Neale Fraser / Maria Bueno	4	3

County Championship Cricket Winners

Yorkshire

1959 saw the 60th officially organised running of the County Championship. Yorkshire won the Championship title ending a seven-year winning streak by Surrey.

Pos.	Team	Pld.	W	L	D	Tie	Pts.
1	**Yorkshire**	**28**	**14**	**7**	**7**	**0**	**204**
2	Gloucestershire	28	12	11	4	1	186
3	Surrey	28	12	5	11	0	186
4	Warwickshire	28	13	10	5	0	184
5	Lancashire	28	12	7	9	0	184

Test Series Cricket

Australia vs England

Test	Ground	Result
1st Test	Brisbane Cricket Ground, Woolloongabba	Australia won by 8 wickets
2nd Test	Melbourne Cricket Ground, Melbourne	Australia won by 8 wickets
3rd Test	Sydney Cricket Ground, Sydney	Match drawn
4th Test	Adelaide Oval, Adelaide	Australia won by 10 wickets
5th Test	Melbourne Cricket Ground, Melbourne	Australia won by 9 wickets

New Zealand vs England

Test	Ground	Result
1st Test	Lancaster Park, Christchurch	England won by an innings and 99 runs
2nd Test	Eden Park, Auckland	Match drawn

England vs India

Test	Ground	Result
1st Test	Trent Bridge, Nottingham	England won by an innings and 59 runs
2nd Test	Lord's Cricket Ground, London	England won by 8 wickets
3rd Test	Headingley, Leeds	England won by an innings and 173 runs
4th Test	Old Trafford , Manchester	England won by 171 runs
5th Test	Kennington Oval, Kennington	England won by an innings and 27 runs

The Indian cricket team toured England during the summer of 1959. The team played five Test matches against England and lost them all: this was the first time that England had won all the Tests in a five-match series.

THE COST OF LIVING

Ask a Bristol smoker and he'll tell you why Bristol is today's cigarette. Its Multicel tip (so firm, so clean) lets the full, cool flavour of fine tobacco through for the kind of smoking only Bristol smokers know. Just ask a Bristol smoker.

Today's cigarette is a BRISTOL

BRISTOL
TIPPED CIGARETTES

FULL SIZE **3/4** FOR 20—1/8 FOR 10

COMPARISON CHART

	1959 Price	1959 (+ Inflation)	2018 Price	% Change
3 Bedroom House	£3,450	£76,887	£227,874	+196.4
Weekly Income	£7.15s.7d	£173.37	£535	+208.6
Pint Of Beer	1s	£1.11	£3.60	+224.3
Cheese (lb)	3s.2d	£3.53	£3.38	+4.2
Bacon (lb)	3s.9d	£4.18	£3.34	-20.1
The Beano	2d	19p	£2.50	+1215.8

FREARS

biscuits keep crisper longer

—if I let them !

Yes, Frears biscuits stay really fresh and crisp in their double-wrapped airtight packets. There are lots of delicious varieties and some wonderful assortments from which to choose.
Ask your grocer for Frears biscuits today.

'Tea Time' is one of Frears' most popular assortments. Buy them in an airtight ½ lb. packet or loose from a tin.

FREARS LIMITED · WOODGATE · LEICESTER

SHOPPING

Chivers Olde English Marmalade (1lb jar)	1s.6d
Knorr Tomato Soup (6 servings)	1s.6d
Camp Coffee (large)	5s.9d
Huntley & Palmers Breakfast Biscuits (pkt.)	1s.6d
Macfarlane Lang Granola Digestive Biscuit (pkt.)	11½d
McVitie's Digestive Biscuits (½lb pkt.)	11½d
Milky Way	3d
Dascote Headache Tablets (large box)	4s.8d
Body Mist Deodorant (small)	3s.6d
Librox Denture Fixative	1s.2d
Elastoplast Pocket Strips	1s
Persil Washing Powder (giant size)	1s.11d
Squeeze-On Kleenoff Oven Cleaner	2s.8d
Spratts Dog Meat (large size)	1s.11d

CLOTHES

Women's Clothing

Barkers Unlined Coat	£3.19s.6d
Fairway House Winter Housecoat	£1.15s
Garlaine Sleeveless Silk Finish Cotton Suit	11gns
Roecliff & Chapman Nylon Organza Dress	15½gns
Ex-WRAF Ladies Overalls	12s.11d
Pure 100% Wool Long Sleeve Pullover	8s.11d
Lee Cooper Cavalry Twill Slacks	£1.15s
Gamages Cotton-Pretty Playtex Bra (x2)	£1.8s.6d
J.B. All Stretchable Breath-In-Bra	17s.6d
Enturine Panel Action Girdle	£1.15s
New Ex-Wrens Panties (2 pairs)	9s.11d
Portland Sandal Shoes	£2.19s.11d
Real Sheepskin Mitts	10s.6d

Men's Clothing

Burberry Weathercoat	8½gns
Officers Regulation Trench Coat	£2.4s.9d
Superfine Poplin Shirt (x3)	8s.6d
Tootal Tie	from 5s
Relax-Sirs All Weather Slacks	£2.17s.6d
Anden Corduroy Trousers	£1.9s.11d
Ex-Govt. All Wool Pants	5s.6d
Invicta Striped A-Front Briefs	6s.11d
Ex-British Army Long Pants	7s.6d
British Army Boots	15s.6d
George Webb Suede Shoes	£2.19s.9d

Here it is!

The most exciting styling ever
—straight from the world's
fashion centres...

Lee Cooper

Cavalry Twill SLACKS

You'll adore the easy casual air, sleek tailored fit of these
new style slacks, and the fabric too.
It's highly mercerised 100% cotton cavalry twill—
easy-to-care-for, washes and washes,
wonderfully good looking and in such lustrous colours.
Make sure you see this newest brilliant idea
from Lee Cooper. Shades: oriental red, electric blue,
desert sand or black. Sizes 22″-32″.

PRICE 35/-

Also available in Junior Miss

Lee Cooper's

NEW Campus CASUALS

Sleek American-inspired styling
for you in ribbed Bedford cord, with
attractive P.V.C. piping.
Shade: Desert sand. Sizes 22″-30″.

PRICE 27/6

Also available in Junior Miss

Available from
your local
Stockist

LEE COOPER LTD., Faringdon Avenue, Harold Hill, Romford, Essex

58

TOYS

15 Inch Plastic Helicopter	8s
Hoover Toy Cleaner	£1.5s
Realistic Machine-Gun On Tripod	15s
Toy Piano	9s.6d
Clockwork Train Set	9s.6d
Wagon Train Shooting Game	5s.3d
Airfix Constant Scale Construction Kit	from 2s
Plastic Model Racing Car	5s
13 Inch Little Beauty Vinyl Doll	17s.6d
Jacko The Lovable Monkey	15s.6d
Lotto Bingo Game	2s.6d
Set Of Skittles	7s.6d
Wheeled Shopping Basket	3s.9d
Beetle Drive Family Game	4s.6d
Ludo Board Game	2s
Cement Mixer Lorry	2s
Plastic Tea Set	4s
Paint Box	1s
Assorted Balloons	6d

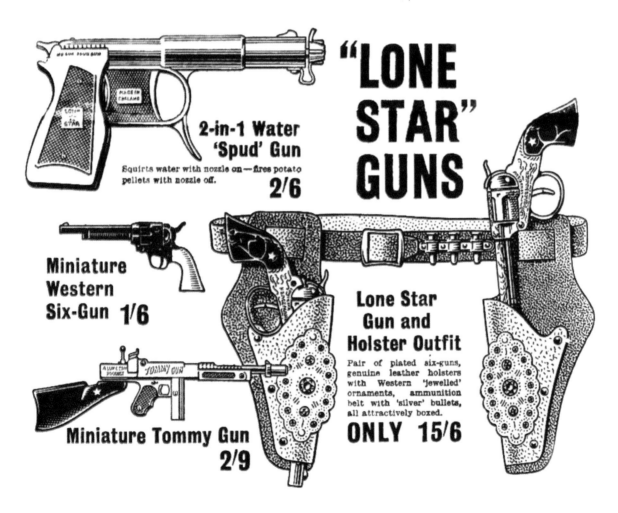

2-in-1 Water 'Spud' Gun

Squirts water with nozzle on — fires potato pellets with nozzle off.

2/6

"LONE STAR" GUNS

Miniature Western Six-Gun 1/6

Miniature Tommy Gun 2/9

Lone Star Gun and Holster Outfit

Pair of plated six-guns, genuine leather holsters with Western 'jewelled' ornaments, ammunition belt with 'silver' bullets, all attractively boxed.

ONLY 15/6

ELECTRICAL ITEMS

Ultra 21 Inch Television Set (B&W)	75gns
His Master's Voice 17 Inch Television Set (B&W)	63gns
Popular Tape Recorder	16gns
Electrolux Refrigerator	£47.17s.5d
Burco Boiler-Wringer Washing Machine	£29.0s.7d
Nortic Washing Machine	£16
Morphy-Richards Super-Suction Vacuum Cleaner	£24.4s.3d
Consort Vacuum Cleaner	£6.6s
Singer 'Re-Built' Electric Sewing Machine	£8.7s.6d
Kodak Home Projector	9gns
Philishave Jet Rotary Action Electric Shaver	£7.7s
Bridges Neonic Drilll	£7.19s.6d

OTHER PRICES

Aston Martin DB MkIII Saloon Car	£3076.7s
Vauxhall Velox Car	£983.17s
Morris Mini Minor Car	£497
BEA All-In Holiday To Paris (8 days)	from £26
Voyagers Fully Inc. Holiday To Majorca (11 days)	from 36½gns
Rhine River Cruise On The M/V Regina (10 days)	from 28gns
Cooks Holiday To The Italian Riviera (2 weeks)	from £45.18s
Queen Anne Style Polished Kidney Dressing Table	£3.19s.6d
27in Wool Pile Wilton Carpet (per yd.)	26s.11d
Ranbury Concrete Garage	£46.15s
RotoGardener Rotavator	£44
Qualcast Panther Roller Mower	£8.12s.6d
Warma Paraffin Heater	£12.10s.9d
Monobright Oil Heater	£11.16s
Royal Portable Typewriter	£23.10s
Knitmaster Popular Knitting Machine	£15
H. Samuel Heart Design Diamond Engagement Ring	£14
H. Samuel 22ct. Gold Wedding Ring	£3.2s.6d
Whitehall Supplies Shockproof Pocket Watch	£1
Johnnie Walker Red Label Whisky	£1.17s.6d
Cinzano Bianco (large bottle)	8s.10d
Partners' Finest Rich Ruby Port	£1
Stones Original Ginger Wine	8s.6d
Babycham (24 bottle case)	£1.10s
Player's Bachelor Cigarettes (20)	3s.4d
Vanity Fair Magazine	1s.6d
Women's Realm Magazine	4d

MONEY CONVERSION TABLE

Old Money		Equivalent
Farthing	¼d	0.1p
Half Penny	½d	0.21p
Penny	1d	0.42p
Threepence	3d	1.25p
Sixpence	6d	2.5p
Shilling	1s	5p
Florin	2s	10p
Half Crown	2s.6d	12.5p
Crown	5s	25p
Ten Shillings	10s	50p
Pound	20s	£1
Guinea	21s	£1.05

Do you know your Oysters . . ?

It takes an expert to distinguish between different varieties of oyster. But there's nothing like a Guinness — as you will readily recognise — especially with shellfish of any kind.

(The four oysters are: COLCHESTER, DUTCH, PORTUGUESE and WHITSTABLE, reading from the top in a clockwise direction).

...and how good GUINNESS is with Oysters

One of the most advanced cars you can buy to-day!

THE BRILLIANT

with Automatic Transmission

There's no mistaking the air of distinction about the Riley Two-Point-Six, the long, low build and the whisper-quiet 6 cylinder engine. But you respect it most of all when you feel the sparkling acceleration, the wonderful cornering and power-assisted brakes. Like its forerunners, the Riley Two-Point-Six is built by enthusiasts for enthusiasts. And what spacious luxury it offers: real leather upholstery, polished walnut finish, two-tone styling and many other Riley refinements.

£940 *plus* £471.7s. P.T.

See and try the Riley Two-Point-Six at your nearest Riley Dealer's showrooms. Available with overdrive or completely automatic transmission as optional extras.

The lively Riley One-Point-Five. This is the compact four seater Riley with the big performance and low running cost.

£575 *plus* £288.17s. P.T.

Riley for Magnificent Motoring

Every RILEY carries a 12 MONTHS' WARRANTY and is backed by Europe's most comprehensive service—B.M.C.

RILEY MOTORS LTD., Sales Division, COWLEY, OXFORD
London Showrooms: 55/56 Pall Mall, S.W.1   Overseas Division: Nuffield Exports Ltd., Oxford and 41/46 Piccadilly, W.1

R 103

CARTOONS

Printed in Great Britain
by Amazon

44582609R00039